Your Skin Holds You In

MESSNER BOOKS BY HELEN DOSS
Your Skin Holds You In
All the Better to Bite With

YOUR SKIN HOLDS YOU IN

by Helen Doss

*Illustrated with Drawings by Christine Bondante
and Photographs*

Julian Messner

New York

Copyright © 1978 by Helen Grigsby Doss
All rights reserved including the right of reproduction in whole or in part in any form. Published by Julian Messner, a Simon & Schuster Division of Gulf & Western Corporation, Simon & Schuster Building, 1230 Avenue of the Americas, New York, N.Y. 10020.

Manufactured in the United States of America

Design by Philip Jaget

PHOTO CREDITS
Eli Lilly and Co., p. 8
Jack C. Henderson, pp. 28, 61
Anne Keefe, pp. 23, 30, 38, 57
Lion Country Safari, Stockbridge, Georgia, pp. 14, 34
National Dairy Council, p. 61
Tucson School District 1, pp. 11, 25, 26, 37, 45

Library of Congress Cataloging in Publication Data

Doss, Helen Grigsby.
   Your skin holds you in.

   Includes index.
   1. Skin—Juvenile literature.   2. Skin—Care and hygiene—Juvenile literature.   I. Title.
QP88.5.D67   612'.79   78-2777
ISBN 0-671-32935-9

CONTENTS

	INTRODUCTION—YOUR AMAZING SKIN	7
1	HOW YOUR SKIN GROWS	10
2	THE INSIDE OF YOUR SKIN	14
3	KEEPING COOL, KEEPING WARM	19
4	THE COLOR OF YOUR SKIN	24
5	YOU FEEL WITH YOUR SKIN	29
6	YOUR HAIR GROWS OUT OF YOUR SKIN	34
7	FINGERNAILS AND TOENAILS	39
8	THINGS THAT BITE, STING, OR BLISTER YOUR SKIN	44
9	HELP FOR HURT SKIN	49
10	HAVE HEALTHY SKIN!	56
	GLOSSARY	62
	INDEX	64

DEDICATED TO
AN ARTIST FRIEND WHO ILLUSTRATED MY LAST BOOK
CHARLES CLEMENT
AND TO HIS TALENTED NIECE
CHRISTINE BONDANTE
WHO ILLUSTRATED THIS ONE

The author wishes to express her thanks to:

Peter Lynch, M.D. Head of the Department of Dermatology at the University of Arizona Medical School; Rodney S. W. Basler, M.D., of the Department of Dermatology at the University of Arizona Medical School; Robert P. Friedman, M.D., dermatologist in private practice in Tucson, Arizona; Dr. Frederick S. Hulse, Professor of Anthropology, University of Arizona;

for providing material and for giving of their time to read the manuscript.

INTRODUCTION
Your Amazing Skin

Your skin fits you, with very few wrinkles.

Wiggle your fingers. Make funny faces. Move your arms and legs in all directions. You see, your skin is elastic. It stretches out, and returns to shape, like a rubber band. And as you grow, your skin grows with you.

Your skin is waterproof, washable, and tough.

Wiggle your fingers. Make funny faces. Your skin is elastic and stretchable.

Your skin holds you in. It wraps around you, and protects your bones, muscles, and other organs. An *organ* is a part of the body organized to do a particular job. Your skin is the largest organ of all. And, like all organs, the skin has its own special work to do.

Your skin keeps growing as long as you live. During most of your life, it fits you very well. But, as people get older, skin begins to sag and fit more loosely. Skin on an older person does not snap back quickly and gets more creases and wrinkles in it.

Besides its job of holding you in, skin keeps germs and dirt out. Your skin is tough, waterproof, and washable, and so it is an important defense against disease.

With the help of your skin, your body is able to stay at an even, healthy temperature. It has ways to warm you on a cold day. On a very hot day, it helps cool you.

Your skin is also a busy factory. When you go out into the sunlight, your skin gets busy and makes *melanin,* a coloring material. Melanin helps protect you from the harmful rays of the sun. Your skin also uses sunshine to make Vitamin D for strong bones and teeth. Your skin makes oils and hair and nails, and even new skin. Skin can usually repair itself, too, when it is cut or burned or scraped.

Your skin is useful and amazing. It's fun to learn more about it.

CHAPTER 1
How Your Skin Grows

FROM ONE CELL TO MANY

You began life as one very tiny *cell,* the basic matter of all living things. This cell divided into two cells, which grew and divided again, and again, and again, until there were millions of cells. Somewhere along the way, the cells became specialized—they became a particular kind of cell. They became heart cells, blood cells, muscle cells, bone cells, skin cells.

Cells that were alike banded together and became *tissue.* Skin cells form skin tissue, for example. There are different kinds of skin cells, so there are different kinds of skin tissue. There are hair and nails and the skin that holds you in.

These different kinds of tissue work together to perform particular jobs in the body, and are called *organs.* Your skin is your largest organ, and its main job is to protect other organs like your eyes, your heart, your lungs, your stomach.

YOUR SKIN KEEPS GROWING ALL YOUR LIFE

Cells do not live forever. Your body keeps producing replacement cells throughout your life for most of your organs. Thousands of dead cells are being shed by your skin every minute. But since the cells are so tiny, you can't feel or see it happening! Nor do you feel your skin adding new cells. It takes about a month for every skin cell to die and be replaced.

A snake gets too big for its skin, and grows a new skin underneath. Then it wiggles out of the old skin. You lose your old, outside skin, too. But it doesn't come off in one piece. Every day you are shedding thousands of dead, outer skin cells!

The cells on the outside of your skin are dead. But just underneath these dead cells are living, growing cells, slowly moving to the outside. As the live cells come near the top of your skin, they get flatter. And they begin to die. By the time you can see them, they are flat and dead. This layer of dead or hardened cells is about as thin as a page of this book. And it flakes off. After a swim or bath, or when you take off a bandage, have you sometimes noticed the flaky skin ready to fall or be rubbed off? Or have you seen anyone with dandruff? Dandruff is a name given to dead skin cells that have flaked off from the scalp in large amounts.

YOUR SKIN GROWS WITH CREASES, RIDGES, HAIRS, AND HOLES

Curl your hand into a cup shape. See how deep creases help to fold away extra skin on your palm and fingers?

Stretch out your palm and study it in bright light. Can you see many more smaller creases and crisscross lines? These help the skin to stretch and fold when you open and close your hands.

Now look for very small, curving rows of lines and ridges in the skin on your hand, especially at the fingertips. Scientists call them *friction ridges,* but you call them *fingerprints*. They help you to pick up and hold things better. Your fingerprints are different from those of any other human being. That is why fingerprints can be used to identify a person.

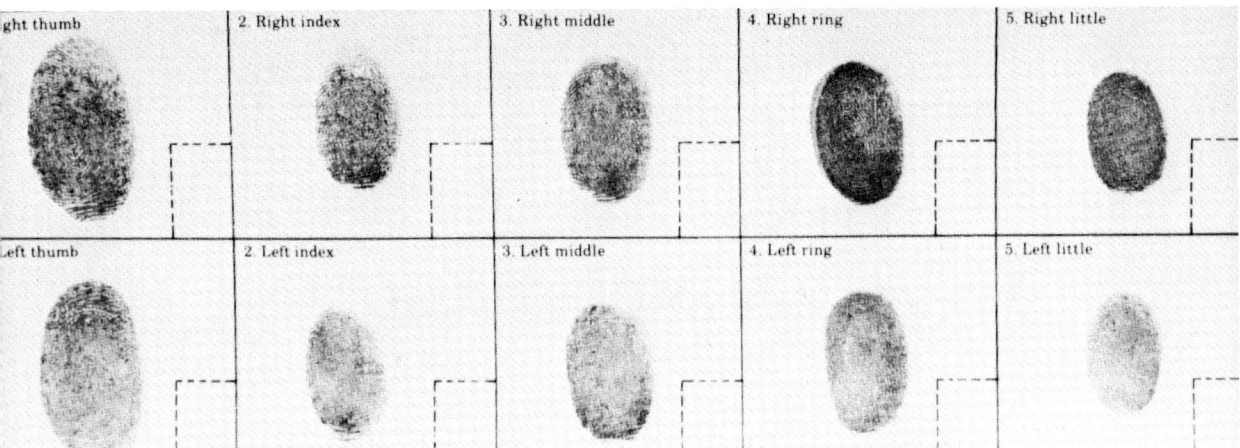

Each of your fingerprints is different. On each fingertip, the lines—or friction ridges—curve, swirl, or loop in different patterns. Nobody in the world has patterns of friction ridges exactly like yours.

Look at your arms and legs, or the backs of your hands. Can you see the tiny hairs there? Each of the hairs on your body grows out of the skin through a tiny opening, called a *follicle. Sebum* (see'-bum) also comes out of these follicles. Sebum is an oil for your skin and hair.

Follicles are not the only openings in your skin. If you have a magnifying glass, look at the back of your hand or the skin on your arm. You will see many more holes in the spaces between the hair follicles. These are your *pores*. The pores are the open ends of tiny tubes called sweat glands. Some waste materials, things the body does not need, are released through the pores. The waste material is mostly water, with a little salt and other chemicals. We call it *sweat* or *perspiration*. Sweat helps cool your skin.

CHAPTER 2
The Inside of Your Skin

Your skin is thicker in some places than in others. Take a pinch of skin at the back of your neck, then at the inside of your wrist. Which one is thicker? The bottoms of your feet have the thickest skin. They carry all your weight. Where do you think the skin is thinnest? Did you guess your eyelids?

Whatever its thickness, all skin is divided into two different layers.

*Some of the thickest skin among animals is found on the pachyderms. This name comes from two greek words—*pachy *(thick) plus* derm *(skin). This hippopotamus, along with the elephant and the rhinoceros, is a pachyderm.*

YOUR THIN EPIDERMIS

The epidermis is the protective cover of your skin, with hard, flat, dead cells on top. There are no blood vessels in this layer. If you bleed, it is because you have scraped off the epidermis, or cut through it.

In the lower part of the epidermis new cells are always being born and moving upward, pushing older cells toward the top.

These growing and dividing cells are full of *protein.* Protein makes up most of the body of the cell. As the cells die, their protein dries up and the cell becomes hard. By the time the cell has reached the top of the epidermis the protein has become hornlike and tough. This is what makes your skin smooth, strong, and washable.

Sometimes, though, extra dead cells build up where your skin is exposed to repeated pressure. The dead cells clump together instead of falling off. This is called a *callus,* or, if it's on a toe, a *corn.* You may get a callus on your finger from a lot of writing with your pencil or pen. If you go barefoot, you'll have calluses on the bottom of your feet.

THE THICK AND BUSY LAYER—YOUR DERMIS

The bottom layer of your skin, the *dermis,* is much thicker than the epidermis. All its cells are alive.

There are many *blood vessels* in your dermis. They bring in food that the cells need, and they carry away waste products.

Your dermis also has many branching nerves. *Nerves* are tiny soft fibers that act like telephone wires to carry messages to and from your brain to all parts of your body. The nerves in the dermis carry messages about heat, cold, pressure or touch, and pain.

Deep inside the dermis, the hair follicles hold your *hair roots.* Hair is everywhere on your skin, except for the palms of your hands and the soles of your feet.

There are glands in your dermis also, glands that make sebum, and sweat glands. There are also some fat cells in your dermis.

CROSS SECTION OF SKIN (SIMPLIFIED)

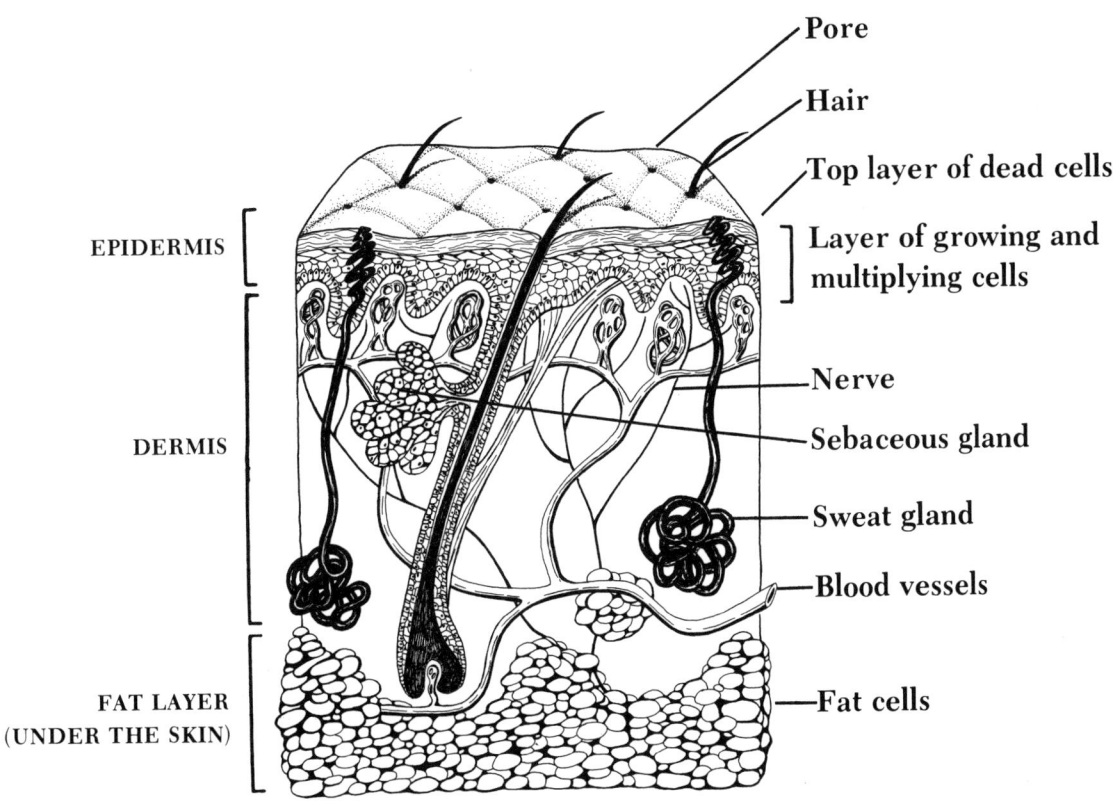

The thick dermis layer is full of the "working parts" of your skin. It is like a cake which is very bumpy on top. Over it lies the thin epidermis, like an icing or thin frosting, fitting down into all the bumps and hollows of the dermis.

UNDER YOUR SKIN

On most parts of your body, there is a layer of fat under the skin.

But touch your eyelids—almost no fat under this thin skin. Tap on top of your head. A bony skull protects your brain, so that little fat-padding is needed there.

Pinch your abdomen, below your waist. Can you feel the fat padding under the skin? If you are overweight, this fat gets very thick.

Feel the cushion of fat where you sit down. This fat protects the bones and muscles and makes sitting more comfortable.

Feel the parts on the bottom of your feet, the edges of your palms, and your fingertips. Can you feel soft, protective cushions of fat there?

CHAPTER 3
Keeping Cool, Keeping Warm

YOUR SKIN HELPS TO KEEP YOU WARM

When the weather turns cold, the fat layer under your skin is very helpful. Fat gives you *insulation,* a barrier against the cold.

If you get chilled, your skin nerves send a message to your muscles. Whether you want to or not, your muscles begin to shiver and shake. This shivering movement builds up the heat inside you.

Your coat and hat and scarf—and your skin—help keep you warm in cold weather. But when the temperature is very low, skin can freeze. It turns grey and numb. This is called frostbite. Frostbitten skin can die. It must be carefully treated.

At the same time, the blood moves away from the skin surface. More blood circulates deep inside your body to warm you. The skin nerves also tell the muscles to shut all openings—pores and hair follicles. The muscle fibers act like a drawstring, making little bumps all over the skin. These are the "goose pimples" or "gooseflesh" we know so well.

HOW YOUR SKIN KEEPS YOU COOL

When you get too hot, the blood vessels in your skin *expand,* get bigger. Much more blood flows toward the

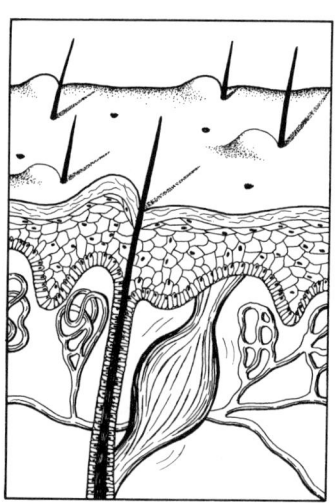

A cross-section of skin when it is cold. Blood vessels are very small. The skin is paler. When furry animals get cold, all the hairs are pulled upright, trapping more warm air next to the skin. Your body hairs are too tiny to trap air, but they still pull upright when the skin is chilled. This pushes up a bump in the skin, next to each hair—"goose-bumps" or "goose-pimples." Feeling afraid or on your guard can cause the same thing in the skin. People say things like "I felt a chill of fear!" "It was enough to make my hair stand on end!"

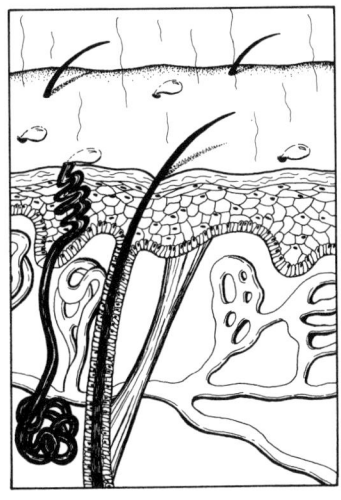

A cross-section of hot skin. Blood vessels are large, making the skin looked flushed and red. Sweat glands pour more water onto the skin, to cool it. The same things happen when you get embarassed, or very angry. Your face blushes red. People say, "Now don't get so hot and bothered!"

surface of your skin. This blood carries heat from deep inside your body. To help the heat leave the body, the skin opens all its pores wider. The sweat glands pour out more sweat. The sweat dries on your skin. This cools you, which makes you more comfortable on a hot day. On a cold day, if you perspire from too many clothes, you may get chilled.

To see how this works, wet one hand with cool water. Now wave both hands in the air. Which feels cooler—the wet hand or the dry one?

FEELING COOLER ON A HOT DAY

When the weather is sizzling hot, you can help your skin to keep you cool.

Try to do only quiet things. Remember that muscle activity builds up extra heat in your body.

If you go outside, wear loose, lightweight clothes to protect your body from the sun's heating rays. White or light-colored clothes don't absorb as many of these rays as dark colors do, and so are cooler to wear. A hat shades and protects your head.

A dog cannot perspire all over its body, as you do. Perhaps this is a good thing, or its fur would be soaked in hot weather. A dog pants, letting water drip and evaporate from its tongue. A dog also sweats through the pads of its feet.

Water helps you to feel cooler in hot weather.

Indoors, bare feet are cooler. Outdoors, canvas tennis shoes or open sandals let perspiration evaporate. Cotton socks are better for sweaty feet than nylon socks.

Drink water often. Your body needs it to replace the large amounts that your skin is sweating away.

A long, cool bath or a shower helps your skin feel cooler. So does a swim or playing outside under a shower from the sprinkler.

CHAPTER 4

The Color of Your Skin

PEOPLE ARE ALL ONE COLOR—IN DIFFERENT SHADES

The color of your skin—and of everybody else's—comes from different mixtures of melanin and carotene, and from your blood.

The skin under your nails is pink in color, because of the blood vessels very close to the surface. Press down on the tips of your fingers and watch them get pinker and whiter.

Your skin may take on a rosy tone when you blush or when you have been very active. The thinner skin is, and the lighter it is, the more pink shows through.

Carotene is in the body in very small amounts. Mostly, it colors the soles of your feet and the palms of your hands a slightly yellowish color. There is also a little carotene in the eyes.

Different mixtures of color in the skins of these artists, as well as in their drawings!

Melanin is the main coloring material in the skin. It is dark brown. Everyone has inherited an amount of melanin which makes their skins different colors, from light cream to very dark brown. Melanin also darkens the hair and eyes. Only *albinos,* people whose skin and hair are very white, have no melanin.

A yellow-orange pumpkin has the same coloring material that you have in your skin—but more of it!

WHEN THE SUN SHINES ON YOUR SKIN

Sunlight causes your melanin-making cells to become more active. More dark melanin is made. This colors your skin, making a "tan."

Too much sun, too fast, can burn the skin. It hurts, itches, and feels very hot. Large watery blisters may form. Afterwards the outer skin peels or flakes off.

Many doctors today think that sunburning and tanning are bad for skin over the years. By middle age, skin cancers can begin to form. This is the most common cancer in the United States. People with very light skin and

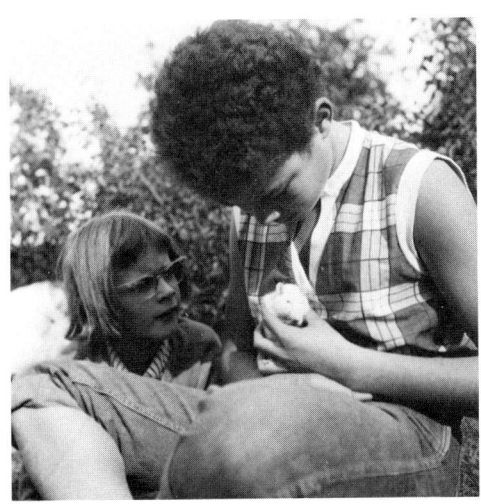

Have you ever seen a white rat? Or a white rabbit? An animal with pure-white skin and hair is an albino. *The eyes also are without color, but they appear pink—because blood color shows through. The few human albinos are the only truly "white" persons!*

Melanin is made in small grains, or granules. If these are scattered evenly in the skin, the skin will be evenly colored. If melanin clumps together more thickly in spots, you will have freckles. Freckles usually show up more on light skin.

hair must protect themselves with hats and sun-screening lotions.

Sunshine does help your body make vitamin D. This is the vitamin you must have for sturdy bones and teeth. The absence of vitamin D can cause a disease called *rickets*. Rickets can cause crippling. But today, milk and many other food products contain added vitamin D for your body to use.

CHAPTER 5
You Feel With Your Skin

Your nerves travel from your brain into all parts of your body, and carry messages back and forth. The millions of tiny nerve endings in your skin give and receive much information about the world around you.

FEELING HOT AND COLD

Some of your skin nerve endings pick up signals of coolness. Others pick up signals of warmth. Long before there were thermometers, people measured temperature by their skin. Have you ever stepped outside and said, "The weather is cooler today," because your skin told you so? Perhaps someone has put a hand on your forehead, and known whether or not you had a fever. You can stick your toe into the water, before a bath or a swim, and tell whether the water is too warm or too cold.

FEELING PAIN

Different nerve endings report pain to you. There are so many, so close together, you can feel a pin-prick anywhere on your skin except where you have a thick callus.

If your pain nerves are just barely tickled, that is what you feel—a "tickle." Get someone to run fingers very lightly over your skin. Or take a couple of loose hairs from your comb or hairbrush, and trail them on your face.

Bother your pain nerves a little more, and it will make your skin feel itchy. Remember your last mosquito bites, or sunburn? Take the eraser end of a pencil, and brush the very tips of your eyebrows backwards. Itchy?

A scraped knee can jangle many pain nerves for a few minutes.

Still more irritation of these same nerve endings will cause real pain. A bad sunburn hurts all over. A small cut hurts, but it won't jangle as many pain nerves as a large scrape, such as a skinned knee.

Believe it or not, you are lucky to have pain nerves. They can keep you from doing damage to your body. Suppose you grabbed hold of a hot pot and didn't feel any pain. Your hand would be badly burned before you knew to take it away. Pain calls attention to injury or disease, so it can be taken care of.

FEELING PRESSURE

As long as they are irritated, your pain nerves keep sending pain messages. Pressure nerves are different. They lie deeper in the dermis. Pressure nerves seem to get tired of sending the same message, and stop—even when the pressure is still there.

This may be a good thing. When you put on shoes, a hat, or a heavy coat, messages report that something is pressing on your skin. If such messages kept bothering your brain, you might have to remove most of your clothes!

But it can also be bad. Too much pressure in one place for too long can cut off the blood circulation and cause the cells there to die.

THE SENSE OF TOUCH

The skin on your palms and fingertips has many touch-nerve endings. Fingertips are so sensitive, they

Touching helps us to tell others we like them.

can recognize smoothness, hairiness, fuzziness, roughness—all kinds of textures and feelings. Blind persons can read by feeling patterns of raised dots on paper.

Your lips also are especially sensitive. Run the side of a pencil along the back of your neck. The touch nerves on the skin of your neck can't tell you very much about the pencil. Now close your eyes, and run the pencil slowly along your lips. The nerves here can tell you the difference in the feel of the wooden part, the eraser, and even the ridges on the metal band holding the eraser.

CHAPTER 6

Your Hair Grows Out of Your Skin

Long ages ago, fish and reptiles developed scales to protect their skin. Birds developed feathers instead. These kept them warm and helped them to fly.

Other animals developed hair or fur from their skin cells. We call these animals *mammals*. Sheep are woolly. Some mammals, like mice, bears, dogs and cats, are quite furry. Human beings are mammals. Sometimes humans are called "naked mammals." Yet you may have a hundred thousand hairs growing from your scalp, and over a million more hairs over the rest of your body! The

You have as many hairs on your body as an ape or monkey. The difference is that your body hairs are shorter, finer, and possibly without much color. But you *can* grow much longer hair on the top of your head.

only place on your body without hair are the palms of your hands and the soles of your feet.

HAIRS GROW, AND HAIRS FALL OUT

You will not see a newly-made hair until it grows above the skin. Even then it may be hard to see, if it is a short, fine, colorless body hair.

Scalp hair will usually stop growing when it gets not much longer than your arm. But sometimes it will grow even longer, or not as long. Boys can grow scalp hair to the same length that girls can. Some people have thick hair, some thin.

It's a good thing that hairs seem to know when to stop growing. If all body hairs just grew and grew, we might get tangled in them.

Human hairs don't grow continuously. Some are growing, some are resting. New ones are always forming. And old ones fall out. A healthy scalp loses many hairs every day. Some you'll find in your comb or hairbrush.

A loose, dead hair doesn't hurt when it falls out. But if you yank a living root from your scalp, you'll feel a sting from your nearest nerve.

Some people, particularly men, lose more hair than is replaced. The possibility of baldness is inherited, but too much falling hair can come from disease or bad eating habits.

HAIR COLOR

Hair gets much of its color the same way that skin does. There are melanin-making cells around the hair root. The darker the hair, the more melanin it has. Pale blond hair has very little melanin.

Sometimes hair has a red pigment, too. Red mixes with different amounts of melanin to make the copper color of a new penny, bright red, or deep auburn.

Skin which is aging usually keeps collecting more melanin. This does not happen with hair. The cells around the hair roots sometimes slow down or stop making melanin. Hair gradually becomes colorless, looking gray or white.

Hair doesn't always stay the same color. This father's hair once was as light as his son's hair. See if your parents have pictures of themselves when they were very young. Was their hair lighter then? As people grow still older, the hair usually gets lighter again, eventually turning gray or white.

STRAIGHT OR CURLY?

Hair can be as straight as a pencil. It may fall in waves, or loose curls. It could be kinked into very tight curls.

Strangely enough, if you looked at a straight hair through a microscope, you would see that it looked very round. But the curlier a hair is, the more flat it is—like a ribbon. Little crimps or pinches in it make it bend and curl.

Some who have curly hair want it straightened. They iron it, or use strong chemicals, then pull the hairs straight while they are weakened. This can make the hair dry and brittle, and easily breakable. And as new hair grows in, it is still curly.

Some, born with straight hair, want to make it curly. They get a "permanent wave." This is a chemical treatment which weakens the hair, then puts kinks into it. A "permanent" cannot last, in spite of the name. All the new hair keeps growing in straight.

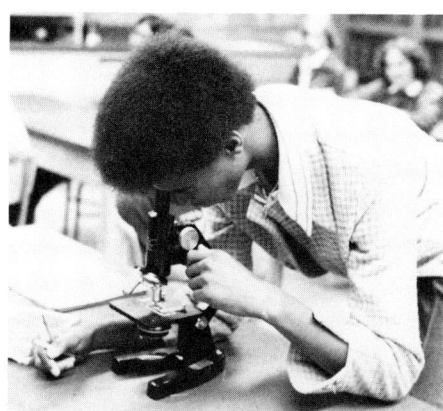

Studied through a microscope, this boy's hair would be seen to be flat, with many pinches and bends.

It could save a lot of time, and possible hair damage, if a hair-style is found which makes the most of *your* hair just as it is, straight or curly.

HAIR CARE

Hair needs combing and a little brushing every day to remove tangles, dust and dirt. Brushing also smooths down the tiny scales which form the outside layer of each hair. And brushing spreads the oil from the skin oil glands all along the hairs, down to the ends. This makes your hair look more attractive and glossy. Too much brushing, however, can harm delicate hair, or make it too oily.

Usually it is enough to wash hair once a week. Use a gentle shampoo, and rinse well. When you reach the teen years, hair and scalp may become so oily that a shampoo is necessary at least twice a week, sometimes daily.

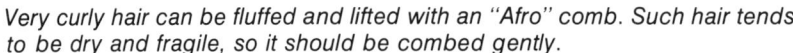

Very curly hair can be fluffed and lifted with an "Afro" comb. Such hair tends to be dry and fragile, so it should be combed gently.

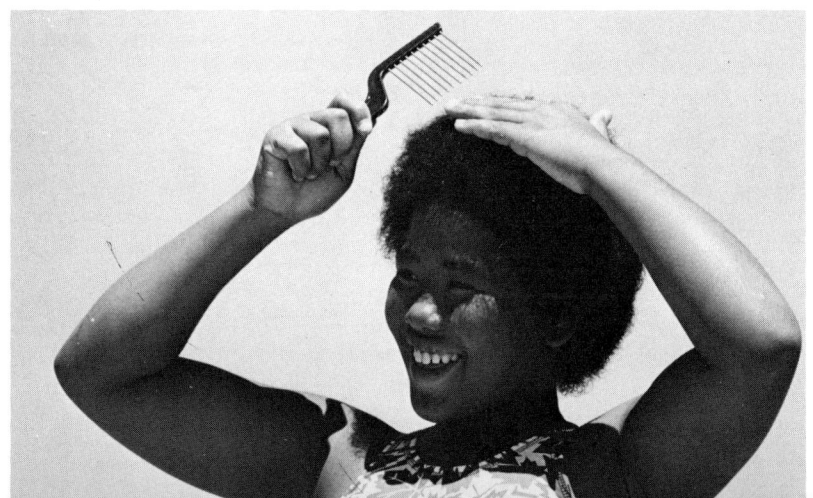

CHAPTER 7
Fingernails and Toenails

Nails are made by skin cells. They are made of the same dried, tough, horny protein material as hair and the outermost skin.

ANIMAL NAILS

Nails are very useful in the animal world.

Have you seen how a parakeet or canary curves its toes and nails around a perch? Perching birds use their nails to help them hang on. Some birds, like chickens and robins, use their toenails to scratch the earth, to uncover a grub or a worm.

A dog uses its nails when it wants to dig a hole, or to scratch itself.

A cat can do something unusual with its nails. Muscles in its paws can retract, or pull back, the nails to protect them. When a cat wants to climb a tree, fight, or catch prey, the long, curved, sharp claws are pushed out.

Animal hoofs are nothing more than big, thick, tough nails. A deer has two toes, ending in a split, or cloven, hoof. A deer can slash and kill snakes with its sharp hoofs. A horse trots on a single toe ending in a hoof. It actually runs tip-toe on its large, horny nails.

Eagles and hawks have long, sharp nails, called talons. With them, birds can catch a mouse or other small animal, and hang on to it.

A horse's large toenail is called a hoof. It does not hurt a horse to have the hoofs trimmed, and an iron horseshoe nailed to the bottom of each hoof. Hoofs, like your nails, are made of dead, horny cells.

Cats, whether pet cats or tigers, have very sharp, retractable claws.

YOUR NAILS

Your nails help your fingers do more things. Try to pick up a pin from a table, using only the sides of thumb and finger. Then see if it is easier if you use your handy nails.

Do you use your fingernails when peeling an orange? When picking a tiny splinter from your skin? How else do you find nails useful?

Nails help to protect the soft ends of your fingers. Have you ever pounded with tacks and a hammer, and hit your thumb? Think how much more mashed your thumb would have been, without that protective thumbnail! In the same way, your toenails protect your toes from bumps and stubbing.

HOW YOUR NAILS GROW

Here is a riddle. What do your fingernails and toenails have, which you also have in your bedroom?

The answer is—a bed. You lie on your bed, and your nails lie upon their nail-bed. The pink skin under your nails is the nail-bed. At the tips, where they come loose from the nail-bed, nails look almost white.

Just like skin, the nails that you see are dead. The live, growing, multiplying cells are under the fold of skin at the base of the nail. As new cells are made, they push ahead onto the nail-bed, moving the old nail cells forward.

Nails grow very slowly compared to hair. It takes from 25 to 30 weeks to grow one inch of new fingernail. For toenails it is even longer—over two years an inch.

NAIL CARE

Fingernails can be trimmed into either a rounded or oval shape, leaving them just long enough to protect the ends of each finger. Rough edges can be smoothed with an *emery board,* a flat stick with emery cloth, a kind of sandpaper, on both sides.

Toenails should always be cut straight across. If toenails are rounded on the sides, edges might be forced

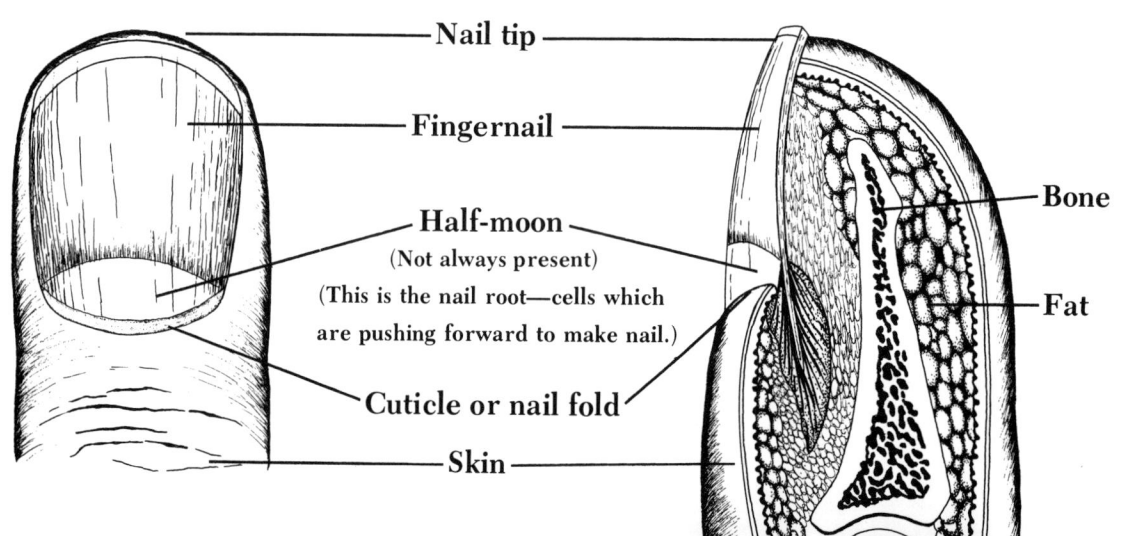

FINGER SEEN FROM OUTSIDE　　　　　**LONGITUDINAL SECTION OF FINGER**

- Nail tip
- Fingernail
- Half-moon (Not always present) (This is the nail root—cells which are pushing forward to make nail.)
- Cuticle or nail fold
- Skin
- Bone
- Fat

downward by the pressure of shoes—especially if shoes or socks are too tight. This can result in a painful condition called "ingrown toenails," and infection easily follows.

Bitten nails are a problem for many. They look bad, but people often fall into a nail-biting habit when bored, lonely, or worried. Talking to someone may help. Sometimes a bad habit lingers on, for no good reason. There are clear coverings that taste bad that can be painted on nails, reminding a nail biter to quit. Nail-biters need to give their minds and hands something better to do so they can enjoy having clean, good-looking, and useful nails.

CHAPTER 8

Things That Bite, Sting, or Blister Your Skin

It's great to be outdoors. Yet in woods and fields, near lakes and rivers, even in your own back yard, living things can attack your skin.

MOSQUITOES

Mosquitoes bother people and animals in the arctic, in the tropics and nearly everywhere else in between. Only females bite and suck blood—they need this blood to develop their eggs.

Two dangerous diseases are carried by certain mosquitoes—malaria and yellow fever. Modern medicine and cleaning up swampy mosquito breeding places have helped curb these diseases.

Put insect repellent on any skin which cannot be covered. Around a campfire, try to sit where the smoke is drifting, because mosquitoes don't like smoke.

Bites feel itchy, but don't let yourself scratch. Scratching can leave larger, infected wounds. Cool the bites with wet cloths. Or try a cool bath with baking soda added. Calamine lotion may soothe itchy bites. A dab of toothpaste feels good, too.

BEES AND WASPS

Bees and wasps don't bite. They wound you with a stinger from the other end.

Wasps—including hornets and yellow-jackets—have longer, more slender bodies than bees. If you're on a picnic, keep meats and ripe fruits covered, until ready to eat. Wasps can smell the goodies, and buzz in for their share. If you stop eating and don't move, they may not attack you.

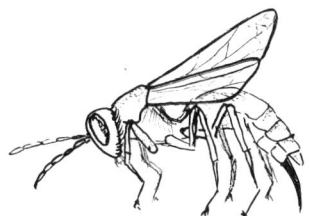

The female wasp has a sharp stinger at the end of her body.

These children are studying bees in their classroom. A drone bee can safely be held in the hand, because it is a male, and males have no stinger. The stinger of a female bee is developed and adapted from an organ once used for laying eggs. It is attached to a poison-sac inside the body. A worker honey-bee has one-way barbs on her stinger. If plunged into tough human or other mammal skin, the barbs hold it while she pumps in her venom. When she flies away, the barb stays, and yanks out the attached poison organs. The bee is more wounded than you are, and she will die. A bumble-bee or a wasp, however, has straight stingers, and can sting again and again.

What if you are stung by a bee or wasp? If a stinger is there, scrape it out with the edge of a knife or your handy fingernail. Ice-cold compresses help ease pain. Some people make a mud pack for the bite.

Bee or wasp venom can sometimes cause very bad allergic reactions. If unusual swelling or sickness begin, the person should be rushed to a doctor.

SPIDERS

Most spiders are harmless. They cannot bite through your tough skin. Their venom is only enough to hurt a fly, and not you. Some spiders are poisonous, though.

The black widow is the best-known poisonous spider. It hides in dark and dusty places, like a woodpile, garage or barn corners. Also poisonous is the brown recluse spider, more slender than the black widow. If either bites

The female black widow has a rounded, shiny black body and pointed legs. Underneath is a red mark in the shape of an hour-glass.

you, you can feel quite sick. Cover the bite with crushed ice wrapped in a wet cloth—and call the doctor or go to a hospital emergency room.

If the spider can be caught, take it with you in a bottle.

ANIMAL BITES

It can be dangerous to tease strange dogs or cats, or to handle wild animals. Stay away from an animal that is acting sick or strange. Dogs, cats, coyotes, skunks, squirrels and bats can carry deadly rabies. Pet dogs and cats should be vaccinated against rabies.

If an animal bites, the wound should be well washed with soap and water, to remove the saliva. Then phone the doctor. Someone should try to trap the animal, or find out where it belongs, so that it can be tested for rabies. If the animal has rabies, or if it can't be found, the bitten person has to be treated for the disease.

POISON OAK AND POISON IVY

Nothing happens when you first touch one of these plants. A day or more later, your skin begins to itch. Tiny blisters form. Calamine lotion helps to soothe the hurt and itchy skin. If the rash is bad, your doctor can help with other remedies.

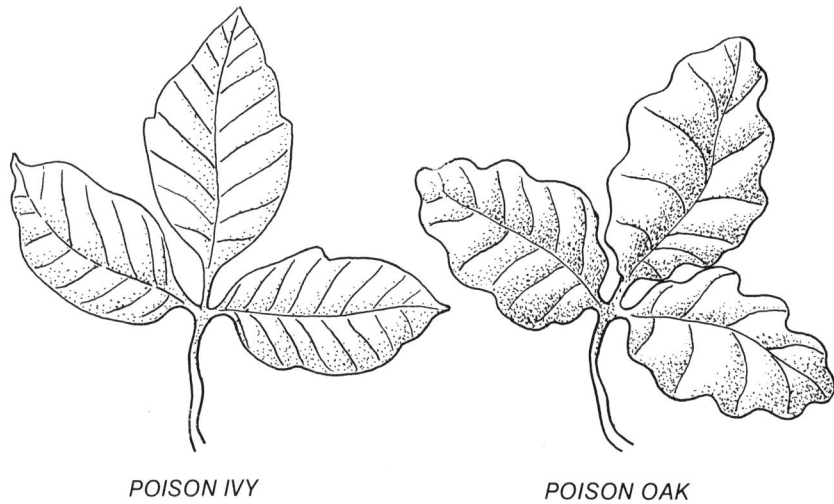

POISON IVY   POISON OAK

There is a useful saying, "leaves three, let them be!" These may be low-growing plants, sturdy bushes, or climbing vines. All parts of the plants contain a poisonous oil—leaves, stems, sap, and the clusters of tiny waxy-white berries. In the fall leaves and berries often turn a beautiful red. Anything brushing against these plants—animal fur, auto or bicycle tires, shoes, or clothing—can transfer the poisonous oil to your skin, even at a long distance from the plants.

What if you unexpectedly blunder into poison oak or ivy? Rush to soap and rinse yourself well, several times. If done within an hour, you may avoid the worst.

Try to learn to recognize the plants from a little distance, and stay away from them. Prevention is much easier than the cure!

CHAPTER 9
Help for Hurt Skin

BRUISES

After a bad bump, your skin can turn "black-and-blue" because tiny blood vessels are broken and have spilled some blood under the skin. There is also some swelling. An icy, wet cloth or cold soak will help reduce the swelling. After a while the color will begin to return to normal as the blood continues to carry away dead cells and clotted blood.

Badly bruised nails turn black because blood has leaked out from broken vessels and has clotted under the skin. Clotted blood has a darker tinge, and reflects still darker from under the skin.

BURNS

Burns are a searing of the flesh. There are three groups of burns, called first-, second-, and third- degree burns. First-degree burns are just a reddening of the skin. No damage has been done to the tissue. Treat it with cold water.

Second-degree burns are more serious, and include blistering. Wet compresses are needed until a doctor can treat the patient.

Third-degree burns are life-threatening. The skin tissue has been destroyed over parts of the body. In such burns, the area must be protected from dust and infection until a doctor can begin treatment. The person should be laid flat, without a pillow, and be covered with a light blanket or sheet until help arrives.

Do not use salves or grease directly on any burn. Cold tea, which contains a substance called tannic acid, is a good first-aid soak for burns.

Most burns could be prevented, just by being careful around flames, and hot things.
Knives are useful for work, especially in the kitchen. They are also fun to use in many hobby crafts. If you learn to use a knife correctly and carefully, you won't cut into your own skin.

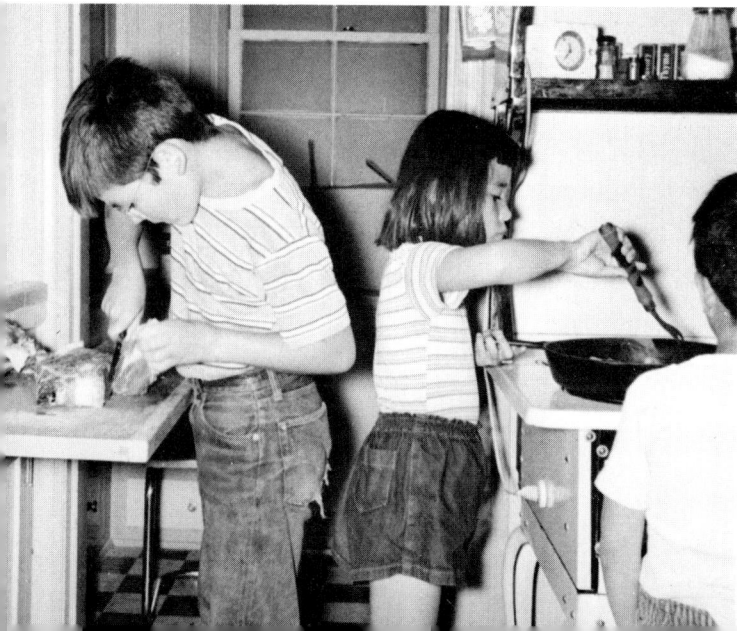

SCRAPES, CUTS, AND PUNCTURE WOUNDS

Soapsuds will disinfect all these wounds. Soap is better than a strong chemical like iodine. Rinse well in cool, running water. If dirt is deeply ground in, let a doctor clean it.

A band-aid will hold the edges of a small cut together. A long or ragged cut may need stitches and a doctor's help.

A deep puncture wound can be dangerous. Nails, teeth, thorns, or splinters can push germs and dirt inside. Squeeze immediately, to make the wound bleed. This helps to cleanse it. If you've not had a tetanus shot recently, see your doctor. Tetanus, sometimes called lockjaw, is a serious disease. The germs of tetanus like to multiply in a deep wound where air cannot reach.

BLACKHEADS, PIMPLES, AND ACNE

As the teen years get closer, the glands work differently. The skin grows more greasy. Blackheads and pimples may appear, especially on the face.

Oil from the oil glands carries dead skin cells up to the surface of the skin. Here they are washed away. Sometimes dead cells, mixed with oil, form a plug, like a cork, in a pore. This darkens on top, from contact with the air, and you have a *blackhead*.

An inflammation of an oil gland makes a *pimple*. This leaking of dead cells and oil into the dermis is very irritating. The top of the skin becomes raised and reddened. Blood vessels bring extra white blood cells to surround the breakout area. *White blood cells* are your body's soldier cells, fighting inflammation and disease.

The material in small blackheads and pimples usually will be pushed out by the skin, and they heal themselves. Squeezing and picking can make them worse.

A continued pimply condition is called *acne*. Your growing-up body is producing sex-hormones, which causes oil glands to be very active. Try some drying acne lotions. If they don't help, see your doctor, or a *dermatologist,* who is a doctor specializing in problems of the skin.

And keep your hands off your face! Break habits of leaning your hands against your chin or cheek. And don't try to *scrub* your face—wash gently.

MOLES

A mole is a growth, flat or raised, and usually dark because of melanin in it. You may be born without any, then get twenty or more as you grow. Most moles are simply left alone. Some people call them "beauty spots."

Ask your doctor to check any mole which begins to change in size or color, or which may be rubbed, scraped, or irritated.

WARTS

A wart is a bump of thick skin, caused by a virus, a germ too small to see. It will often go away by itself. Never chew or pick at a wart, as this can spread new ones. You might want your doctor to remove them for you.

CORNS

A corn is a painful callus on a toe. It is usually caused by a bad-fitting shoe which rubs or presses. A corn plaster will give some relief, or a piece of moleskin, which is a soft, felt-like material with adhesive on the back.

WHAT DO THEY LOOK LIKE INSIDE?

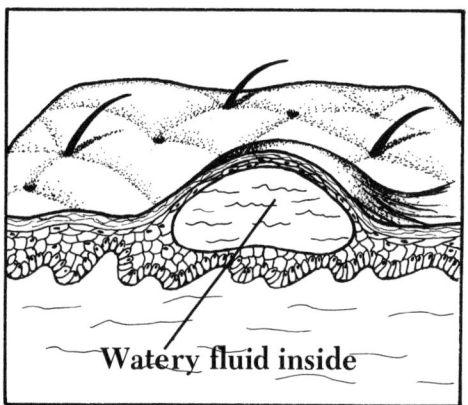

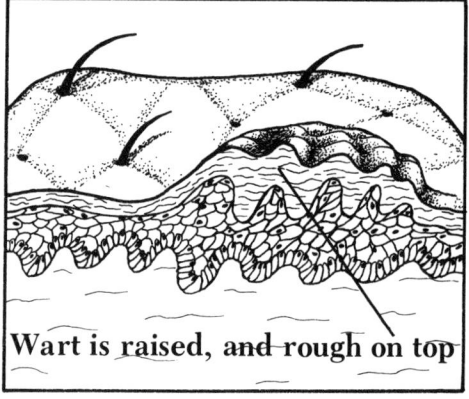

A blister. The skin on top of a blister shows you the thickness of your epidermis. Blisters can be from a burn (including sunburn), from poison oak or ivy, or from friction (as when a shoe rubs a raw spot on your foot). Try not to break a blister. It protects the under layers of skin from infection and loss of needed moisture. Protect with a bandage, and let it open and heal by itself.

A wart. The virus in a wart is too small to see, even with a microscope. The virus causes the epidermis to thicken, and to buckle into very tiny folds. In Mark Twain's books, Tom Sawyer and Huckleberry Finn thought you could cast a spell and make warts go away. Today doctors say that more than half of all warts may begin to dry up, and finally go away, if you really believe they will!

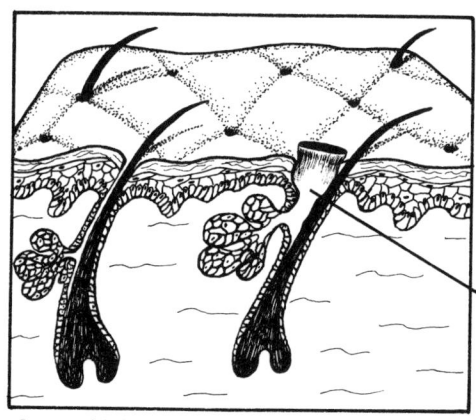

A blackhead. Some thick, waxy oil has hardened, and plugged up a pore. The pore is enlarged. Air makes this greasy plug dark on top.

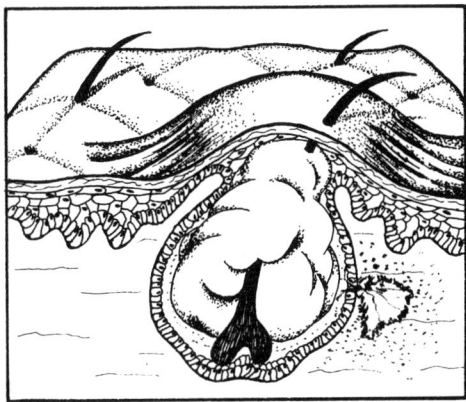

A pimple. *The germs have entered a pore. An infection has started. Blood vessels bring white blood cells, which are the soldiers in your body's constant war on disease to fight the infection. Pus, made up of dead germs and dead white blood cells, forms on top of the skin.*

A boil. *A boil is like a pimple, only there is more of it! The infection causes a very painful swelling. A hard core of dead matter forms in the center. Hot compresses help. They bring more blood, which brings more white blood cells to fight the infection. You can make a boil much worse, if you pinch or squeeze it. When it is ready, it will empty itself. Boils easily spread, unless great care is taken to thoroughly wash hands with soap and water.*

CHAPTER 10
Have Healthy Skin!

For healthy skin, you need to keep it clean and free from injury. You also need to nourish it with good food.

KEEPING YOUR SKIN CLEAN

Every year Americans spend millions of dollars on expensive skin-care products. Yet all you may need is a

The first rule in skin care is cleanliness. Thousands, sometimes even millions, of bacteria live on your skin. When dirt and oil and dead skin cells pile up, they provide food so that these bacteria can multiply.

mild soap, lathered into your face with clean hands and warm water. Always rinse well.

In a city, a film of smog and grime settles on the skin, even if you cannot see it. This mixes with your flaked-off dead skin cells, oil, and stale perspiration. Even in so-called "fresh" country air, dust mixes with your oil, sweat, and dead cells. This daily gummy collection should be washed off every night, before you go to bed. A cool wash in the morning feels refreshing—and helps to wake you up!

Young children, and older adults, usually have little natural oil on their skin. During the teen and young adult years skin tends to get more oily.

For too-oily skin, wash gently with soap several times a day. Never use greasy creams or oily sun-tan lotions. Acne lotion may help.

When skin gets extra-dry, it can look scaly and flaky. Too much water has been lost from the outer cell layers. Avoid long, steamy-hot baths or showers, which draw out moisture. Use very little soap, and luke warm or cool water for washing and rinsing. Pat dry. Then smooth on a little petroleum jelly, baby oil, or dry-skin lotion to help hold in the skin's moisture.

GOOD FOOD FOR HEALTHY SKIN

If you want good health for your body and your skin,

Three ways you can get your daily vitamin D.

you need to eat a healthful variety of foods. Try to cut out, or at least cut down on, candy, sugared drinks, soda pop, doughnuts, cookies, and other popular snack-foods and desserts. Most are far too high in sugar or fat, or both. They also are very low in needed vitamins and minerals.

Vitamin A is especially valuable for skin, and helps you to resist skin diseases. Foods with yellow-orange carotene are very rich in A—carrots, winter squash, egg yolks, fresh or dried apricots, yams and sweet potatoes. Lightly cooked, dark leafy "greens"—like spinach, swiss chard, kale, beet and turnip tops—have needed iron as well as lots of vitamin A.

Several kinds of B vitamins add to skin health. Especially rich are fish, liver, peanuts, eggs, milk, broccoli, and cooked dried beans.

Everybody, but especially growing children, needs daily vitamin D. If there is the right amount of sunshine, your skin will manufacture your vitamin D. Or drink four glasses of vitamin D fortified milk every day. This will give enough calcium for growing bones, too. Cod-liver oil is a good source of vitamin D.

Your living skin needs protein every day. Protein is used to make your millions of new cells, and to repair tissue. Good protein comes from meat, cheese, and eggs.

THE BASIC 4

Still other vitamins, minerals, and energy-foods are needed for good health. How can you know if you will get everything you need?

Look at the Basic 4 chart. At every meal, eat at least one food from each group. If you neglect one group, your body—and your skin—will be weaker. Don't stick to a few favorite foods. Eating, and learning to like, a great variety of foods is a smart plan.

Why not make your own Basic 4 chart? You can use pictures of foods cut from magazines. Or draw and color your own. Put your chart on the kitchen wall or the refrigerator door.

BASIC 4 FOODS

Studies of school lunches show that children waste much food, especially vegetables. The vitamins and minerals which they need get dumped in the garbage! It's just as important to eat basic 4 foods for lunch, as it is for breakfast and dinner. Choose snacks from the basic 4 foods, too!

HOW IT ADDS UP

1. Wash the daily dirt from your skin.
2. Protect your skin from things that might hurt it.
3. If you have light skin, avoid too much sun.
4. Know a little first aid for unexpected skin injuries. See a doctor if you need more help.
5. Eat healthful foods, choosing from the Basic 4 chart.

Doing these things will help you to have healthy and good-looking skin—to hold you in!

GLOSSARY

ALBINO—Any person or animal born with a skin that does not have melanin in it and without the ability to make melanin.

BLACKHEAD—A plugged pore.

CALLUS—A build-up of dead cells that stick together instead of flaking off.

CAROTENE—A yellowish orange substance that gives color to skin. A source of vitamin A.

CELL—The smallest living thing that can move about, feed, grow and reproduce. It is the basic unit of life.

CORN—A callus that grows on the toe.

DERMATOLOGIST—A physician who specializes in the care of skin, hair and nails.

DERMIS—The lower and most important layer of skin.

EPIDERMIS—The top layer of skin.

FINGERPRINT—Tiny even rows of curved ridges and lines that are best seen at the ends of the fingers.

FOLLICLE—The tube in the skin from which a hair grows. It also contains oil glands.

FRICTION RIDGE—See Fingerprint.

INSULATION—Any barrier that controls or stops the flow of heat or cold.

MELANIN—A dark brown pigment that absorbs sunlight and gives skin most of its color.

NAIL BED—The part of the finger or toe on which the nail lies.

NERVE—Fibers that carry messages to and from the brain to all parts of the body.

ORGAN—Any part of the body that is organized to do a particular job.

PIMPLE—Inflamation of an oil gland that makes a bump on the skin.

PORE—A small opening in the skin. Most pores are openings to sweat glands.

PROTEIN—A simple organic foodstuff that gives form to living cells and helps them grow.

PUS—A yellowish liquid made up mostly of dead white blood cells.

SEBUM—Skin oil.

SWEAT GLAND—Tiny tube in the dermis layer, where sweat is made.

TISSUE—A large group of similar cells, collected together.

VITAMIN—One of several kinds of special food substances that the body needs in small amounts to help fight disease and to help get energy from other foods. There are about 26 different vitamins. Vitamins A, D, and several of the Bs are important to skin health.

WHITE BLOOD CELLS—The soldier cells of the body. They fight infection.

INDEX

acne, 52
albino, 26
animal bites, 47
animal nails and hoofs, 39–40
animal skin, 34

basic 4 foods, 69–70
bee stings, 45–46
blackheads, 51–52
blisters, 27, 50
blood vessels, 16, 20, 24, 49, 52
bruises, 49
burns, 9, 31, 49–50

callus, 15, 53
cancer, 27
carotene, 24
cells, 10–12, 15–16, 39, 41–42, 52
color of skin, 24–27
corns, 15, 53
cut skin, 31, 51

dandruff, 12
dead cells, 12, 15, 41, 51, 57
dermatologist, 52
dermis, 16, 31, 52

epidermis, 15

fat, 17–19
fingerprints, 12
fingernails, 39, 41–43, 49
follicles, 13, 16
friction ridges, 12

germs, 9, 51, 53
goose pimples, 20

hair, 9, 16, 34–38; brushing, 38; color, 36; curls, 37; falling, 35–36; growth, 35; roots, 16, 35; shampooing, 38

ingrown toenails, 42–43
insect bites and stings, 44–46
itch, 27, 30, 44, 47

mammals, 34
melanin, 9, 25–27, 36, 52
moles, 52–53
mosquito bites, 44

nails, 9, 39–43, 49, 51; nail-biting, 43
nerves, 16, 29–33
nutrition, 57–60

oil glands, 13, 17, 51–52. *See also* sebum
organs, 8, 10

pain, 16, 29–31
perspiration, 13
pimples, 51–52
poison ivy, 47–48
poison oak, 47–48
pores, 13, 21, 52
pressure, 31
protein, 15, 39, 51
puncture wound, 51

rickets, 28
ridges, skin, 12

sebum, 13, 16, 38, 51–52, 57
shivering, 19
skin, human, 7–9; creases, 12; cleaning, 57; elastic qualities, 7; inside of, 14–18; outside of, 10–13; repair of, 9; thickness, 14–16
spider bites, 46
sunburn, 27, 31, 49
sun-screen lotion, 27
sunshine, 9, 27–28, 59, 61
sweat and sweat glands, 13, 16–17, 21

tanning, 27, 61
tetanus, 51
tickle, 30
tissues, 10
toenails, 39–43; 49
touch, 32–33

virus, 53
vitamin D, 9, 28, 59
vitamins in food, 58–60

wasp stings, 45–46
warts, 53